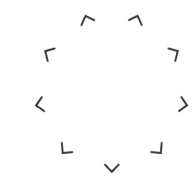

The Generosity Practice

A Four-Session Companion Guide to Help You Experience the Joy of Giving

WaterBrook

John Mark Comer and Practicing the Way

A WaterBrook Trade Paperback Original

Copyright © 2024 by Practicing the Way

Published in the United States by WaterBrook, an imprint of Random House, a division of Penguin Random House LLC.

WATERBROOK and colophon are registered trademarks of Penguin Random House LLC.

Published in association with Yates & Yates, www.yates2.com.

Originally self-published by Practicing the Way (practicingtheway.org) in 2024.

All photos courtesy of Practicing the Way.

Trade Paperback ISBN 978-0-593-60333-8
Ebook ISBN 978-0-593-60334-5

Printed in the United States of America on acid-free paper

waterbrookmultnomah.com

1st Printing

Book and cover design by Practicing the Way

For details on special quantity discounts for bulk purchases, contact specialmarketscms@penguinrandomhouse.com.

Contents

PART 01

Getting Started

Welcome

There is more happiness in giving than in receiving.
—Acts 20v35

Few of Jesus' teachings are more radical, counterintuitive, and disorienting to our cultural assumptions than what Jesus has to say about money and generosity. We hear constantly the Western formula of "more money = more happiness." But Jesus boldly claims that happiness is found not in the accumulation of wealth but in a deeply relational life of giving and love.

We could not be more excited for you to go on this four-session journey of generosity. From a distance, generosity can sound like a hard practice; and it is, at first. But it quickly becomes one of the most joyful of all the practices of Jesus.

Our prayer for the coming weeks is that you begin to discover the great joy Jesus is referring to—not just the good feelings that come from practicing generosity but, ultimately, the joy that comes from participating in the inner life of God himself, the most generous being in all the universe.

May God bless you—richly—as you practice Jesus' way of joyful generosity.

—John Mark Comer and Practicing the Way

How to Use This Guide

A few things you need to know

This Practice is designed to be done in community, whether with a few friends around a table, within your small group, in a larger class format, or with your entire church.

The Practice is four sessions long, with an optional bonus session if you want to go further. We recommend meeting together every week or every other week.

You will all need a copy of this Companion Guide. You can purchase a print or ebook version from your preferred book retailer. We recommend the print version so you can stay away from your devices during the practices, as well as take notes during each session. But we realize that digital works better for some.

Each session should take about one to two hours, depending on how long you give for discussion. See the sample session on the following page.

Are you a group host or facilitator? Read the appendix in the back of this Guide or view our training resources on practicingtheway.org to find information and tips on running this Practice.

Sample Session

Here is what a typical session could look like.

Welcome
Welcome the group and open in prayer.

Introduction (2–3 min.)
Watch the introduction to the session, and pause the video when indicated for your first discussion.

Discussion 01: Practice reflection in triads (15–20 min.)
Process your previous week's practice in smaller groups of three to five people with the questions in the Guide.

Teaching (20 min.)
Watch the teaching portion of the video.

Discussion 02: Group conversation (15–30 min.)
Pause the video when indicated for a group-wide conversation.

Testimony and tutorial (5–10 min.)
Watch the rest of the video.

Prayer to close
Close by praying the liturgy in the Guide or however you choose.

Our Practices are designed to work in a variety of group sizes and environments. For that reason, your gatherings may include additional elements like meals or worship time or may follow a structure slightly different from this sample. Please adapt as you see fit.

The Weekly Rhythm

The four sessions of this Practice are designed to follow a four-part rhythm that is based on our model of spiritual formation.

Learn
about the Way of Jesus.

IN COMMUNITY

Process Together
what is coming up for you through your experience.

WEEKLY   RHYTHM

Practice
with spiritual exercises using your Companion Guide.

ON YOUR OWN

Reflect
on your experience with God.

01 **Learn:** Gather together as a community for an interactive experience of learning about the Way of Jesus through teaching, storytelling, and discussion. Bring your Guide to the session and follow along.

02 **Practice:** On your own, before the next session, go and "put it into practice,"* as Jesus himself said. We will provide weekly spiritual disciplines and spiritual exercises, as well as recommended resources to go deeper.

03 **Reflect:** Reflection is key to spiritual formation. After your practice and before the next session, set aside 10–15 minutes to reflect on

* Luke 8v21.

your experience. Reflection questions are included in this Guide at the end of each session.

04   **Process together:** When you come back together, begin by sharing your reflections with your group. This moment is crucial, because we need each other to process our lives before God and make sense of our stories. If you are meeting in a larger group, you will need to break into smaller subgroups for this conversation so everyone has a chance to share.

Tips on Beginning a New Practice

This Guide is full of spiritual exercises, best practices, and good advice on the spiritual discipline of generosity.

But it's important to note that the Practices are not formulaic. We can't use them to control our individual spiritual formation, or even our relationship with God. Sometimes they don't even work very well. Sometimes throughout this Practice, you might give with the wrong motive: out of compulsion or a desire to be seen. Or you might feel it is impossible to give up certain possessions or resources. That's okay. Our goal isn't to control our spiritual formation but to surrender to Jesus. To give more and more of our deepest selves to him to rescue and save and heal and transform, in his time, in his way, by his power and peace and presence.

The key with the spiritual disciplines is to let go of outcomes and just offer them up to Jesus in love.

Because it's so easy to lose sight of the ultimate aim of a Practice, here are a few tips to keep in mind as you practice generosity.

01 Start small

Start where you are, not where you "should" be. It's counterintuitive, but the smaller the start, the better chance you have of really sticking to it and growing over time.

02 Think subtraction, not addition

Please do not "add" generosity into your already overbusy, overfull life. You are likely already overwhelmed. Instead, think, *How can generosity be lived out through my everyday rhythms and routines? Where do I need to slow down so I can pay more attention to the needs around me? How can I further simplify my life?* Formation is about less, not more. About slowing down and focusing your life around what matters most: life with Jesus.

03 You get out what you put in

The more fully you give yourself to this Practice, the more life-changing it will be; the more you just dabble with it, the more shortcuts you take, the less of an effect it will have on your transformation.

04 Remember the J curve

Experts on learning tell us that whenever we set out to master a new skill, it tends to follow a J-shaped curve; we tend to get worse before we get better. Fewer topics can make us feel more uncomfortable or vulnerable than money. At the start of this Practice, it may feel unnatural or difficult to step more deeply into the generous life, like you are having to pry your heart and hands open. That's okay. Expect it to be a bit difficult at first; it will get easier in time. Just stay with the Practice.

05 There is no formation without repetition

Spiritual formation is slow, deep, cumulative work that happens over years, not weeks. The goal of this four-session experience is just to get you started on a journey of a lifetime. Upon completion of this Practice, you will have a map for the journey ahead and hopefully some possible companions for the Way. But what you do next is up to you.

Before You Begin

A note about the recommended reading

Reading a book alongside the Practice can greatly enhance your understanding and enjoyment of this discipline. You may love to read, or you may not. For that reason, it's recommended but certainly not required.

Our companion book for the Generosity Practice is *Giving Is the Good Life* by Randy Alcorn. Randy is a widely respected author on the subject of God and money and the founder of Eternal Perspective Ministries.

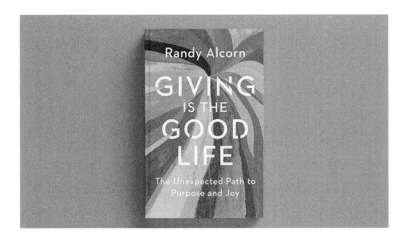

The Spiritual Health Reflection

One final note: Before you begin Session 01, please set aside 20–30 minutes and take the Spiritual Health Reflection. This is a self-assessment we developed in partnership with pastors and leading experts in spiritual formation. It's designed to help you reflect on the health of your soul in order to better name Jesus' invitations to you as you follow the Way.

You can come back to the Spiritual Health Reflection as often as you'd like (we recommend one to two times a year) to chart your growth and continue to move forward on your spiritual journey.

To access the Spiritual Health Reflection, visit practicingtheway.org/reflection and create an account. Answer the prompt questions slowly and prayerfully.

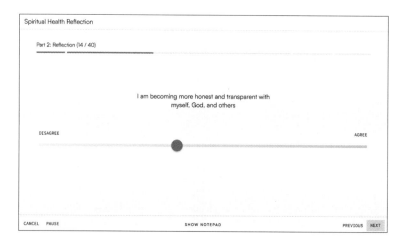

PART 02

The Sessions

SESSION 01

There Is More Joy in Giving Than Receiving

Overview

Jesus' call to generosity is rooted in his vision of God and our place in God's world. In Jesus' teaching on "healthy" versus "unhealthy" eyes,* we are introduced to two strikingly different worldviews—or ways of seeing the world.

Those with an abundance mindset see God as being their Father-provider and the world as teeming with provision and blessing; everything we have is a gift, and there's plenty for all. They live with gratitude toward God and generosity toward neighbor.

Inside this worldview, the radical teachings of Jesus on money and generosity ("Do not worry about tomorrow"; "Freely you have received; freely give"; "Watch out! Be on your guard against all kinds of greed; life does not consist in an abundance of possessions."**) make perfect sense. And we are free to live generously and at peace.

But those with a scarcity mindset see the world as a bleak and godless place of danger; wealth is a zero-sum game; survival of the fittest is the top priority. In this way of "seeing" the world, Jesus' sayings on money sound ludicrous. And we are enslaved to fear and greed.

The practice of generosity is the pathway out—a spiritual discipline by which we index our hearts away from a scarcity mindset to the abundance mindset of Jesus.

---

* Matthew 6v22–23.
** Matthew 6v34, Matthew 10v8, Luke 12v15.

Opening questions

01 What brought you to this Practice? What are you hoping to see God do in your life through it?

02 How were money and generosity handled in your family growing up?

03 What is your primary feeling about money? Fear? Desire for more? Shame? Ambivalence?

04 How do you see generosity as a part of your apprenticeship to Jesus?

Teaching

Scripture

"Do not store up for yourselves treasures on earth, where moths and vermin destroy, and where thieves break in and steal. But store up for yourselves treasures in heaven, where moths and vermin do not destroy, and where thieves do not break in and steal. For where your treasure is, there your heart will be also.

"The eye is the lamp of the body. If your eyes are healthy, your whole body will be full of light. But if your eyes are unhealthy, your whole body will be full of darkness. If then the light within you is darkness, how great is that darkness!

"No one can serve two masters. Either you will hate the one and love the other, or you will be devoted to the one and despise the other. You cannot serve both God and money."

—Matthew 6v19–24

Session summary

- Jesus was right: Happiness is found in the opposite place than where we are often told. There is more happiness in living simply and generously than in acquiring money and possessions.

- A key task of our apprenticeship to Jesus is discovering the joy of living a generous life.

- There are two ways of looking at the world:
  - An abundance mindset
  - A scarcity mindset

- Generosity is a practice by which we index our hearts from a scarcity mentality to the abundance mentality of Jesus.

Teaching notes

As you watch Session 01 together, feel free to use this page to take notes.

Discussion questions

Now it's time for conversation about the teaching. Circle up in triads (groups of three), and discuss the following questions:

01 Whether you were the giver or recipient, share about a time when you experienced the joy of generosity.

02 What fears or desires keep you from being generous? (It could be a scarcity mindset, a need for "security," greed, or something else.)

03 How would your life be different if you were free of the fear of not having enough?

04 What is one act of generosity you can do this week that would counter the fear you may carry?

Practice notes

As you continue to watch Session 01 together, feel free to use this page to take notes.

Closing prayer

End your time together by praying this liturgy:

Father, Provider,
you hold all things in endless,
fearless supply;
help us to live in that trust,
in the rest and extravagance
of knowing we can freely give
in the manner we've received—
selflessly, daringly, lovingly.

Practice

Exercise: Carry out a spontaneous act of generosity.

- Set aside a specific amount of money. It can be a little or a lot, whatever you decide. But before you name an amount, pause and open your heart to God and see if a number comes to mind.

- Take cash out of an ATM to carry with you, or earmark the amount in your debit account to have ready when the right opportunity comes.

- Ask God to give you an opportunity to bless someone.

- Then, just keep your eyes open.

We're not trying to solve global poverty or be heroic in this Practice; we're tapping into the outflow of the Trinity's generous love to all.

Here are a few ideas to spark your imagination:

- Buy coffee or lunch for someone in line behind you.

- Anonymously pay for someone's meal.

- Drop off groceries or a gift to someone who you know is in need or in a time of suffering.

- Send cash digitally to help a friend with medical bills or expenses they can't currently pay.

- Buy a gift for someone to encourage or bless them.

- Give away one of your possessions.

Reach Exercise: Up your spontaneous act of generosity in either frequency or intensity.

We recognize that we're all at different stages of discipleship and seasons of life. To that end, we've added a Reach Exercise to each of the four sessions for those of you who have the time, energy, and desire to go further in generosity.

- **Frequency:** Practice a spontaneous act of generosity two to three times this week, or every day! Whatever you desire. It doesn't have to be expensive or elaborate; just take small, frequent steps into giving.

- **Intensity:** Give in a larger, more sacrificial way. You could take money you've been saving for a large purchase and give some or all of it away to the poor, or you could sell a valuable possession and give to someone in need. We recommend you do this only if you feel a stirring in your heart to give in this way and have the faith to follow the Spirit's gentle invitation.

As you give, watch what happens in your heart.

Go deeper

📖 Read

Giving Is the Good Life by Randy Alcorn
Chapters 01–04 (pages 1–60)

ᴵᴵᴵᴵ Listen

Rule of Life podcast on generosity
Episode 01

◎ Reflect

Reflection is a key component in our spiritual formation.

Millennia ago, King David prayed in Psalm 139v23–24:

> Search me, God, and know my heart;
>> test me and know my anxious thoughts.
> See if there is any offensive way in me,
>> and lead me in the way everlasting.

South African professor Trevor Hudson has quoted one of his pastoral supervisors as saying, "We do not learn from experience; we learn from reflection upon experience."*

If you want to get the most out of this Practice, you need to do it and then reflect on it. Through this simple act, we are learning to pay attention to the movements of the Spirit in our hearts.

---

* Trevor Hudson, *A Mile in My Shoes: Cultivating Compassion* (Nashville, Tenn.: Upper Room Books, 2005), 57.

◎ Reflect

Before your next time together with the group for Session 02, take 10–15 minutes to journal your answers to the questions below.

01   Where did I feel resistance?

02   Where did I feel joy?

03   Where did I most experience God's nearness?

⌨ Discuss (Optional)

For those of you who would like to slow down and integrate this Practice more deeply into your life, we've created four optional group sessions in addition to our video-based sessions.

The Scriptures have so much to say about the generous life that we were not able to include in this Practice. These extra sessions highlight four more key passages and offer discussion questions to provoke deeper Bible study and conversation.

Circle up in a living room or a quiet, relaxed place, read the Scripture together, and enjoy a good discussion using the following pages.

Read this introduction

The Western world, with its consumerist systems and ploys, is designed to make us reach for more, close our grips on what we have, and "look out for number one." Through this Practice, we hope to expose not just the force of this cultural current but the illusion of where it leads: not to a good and wide life but to a smaller one filled with fear, greed, and discontent. In this passage, Paul shows how the upside-down Kingdom has an economy much different from our own. To give is not to lose but to gain. And to live with open hands is to discover a fuller life under a loving Father who is more generous than we can imagine.

Read this Scripture

Remember this: Whoever sows sparingly will also reap sparingly, and whoever sows generously will also reap generously. Each of you should give what you have decided in your heart to give, not reluctantly or under compulsion, for God loves a cheerful giver. And God is able to bless you abundantly, so that in all things at all times, having all that you need, you will abound in every good work. As it is written:

> "They have freely scattered their gifts to the poor;
> their righteousness endures forever."

Now he who supplies seed to the sower and bread for food will also supply and increase your store of seed and will enlarge the harvest of your righteousness. You will be enriched in every way so that you can be generous on every occasion, and through us your generosity will result in thanksgiving to God.

This service that you perform is not only supplying the needs of the Lord's people but is also overflowing in many expressions of thanks to God. Because of the service by which you have proved yourselves, others will praise God for the obedience that accompanies your confession of the gospel of Christ, and for your generosity in sharing with them and with everyone else. And in their prayers for you their hearts will go out to you, because of the surpassing grace God has given you. Thanks be to God for his indescribable gift!

—2 Corinthians 9v6–15

🗨 Discuss (Optional)

Discuss the text

01   Which portion of this passage stands out most to you? Why?

02   In verse 6, Paul likens giving to "sowing." In what ways is generosity like sowing a seed and reaping a harvest?

03   Verse 7 refers to three attitudes around giving: reluctance, compulsion, and joy. Which do you most experience when giving, and how so?

04   Pay attention to the "alls" in verse 8: If we believed this about God, how would it impact the way we relate to our finances and possessions? How do you think our views of God impact our generosity?

Discuss the Practice

01   As you set aside money to give this week, did you experience reluctance or excitement initially? Why?

02   If you're willing, can you share about the instance(s) of how you used the money to bless someone?

03   How did the person you helped respond, and how did their reaction affect you?

04   After this week's practice, how did you personally experience the connection between "sowing generously" and "reaping generously" from 2 Corinthians 9?

SESSION 02

Watch Out for Greed!

Overview

"The more you *get*, the more you *want*." Few truths cut more deeply across the breadth of the human experience. No matter how much money or stuff we amass, we never feel like we have enough.

Even more haunting: "The more we get, the more neurotic we often become." Jesus' counterintuitive insight is this: Not only does wealth not make us happy (beyond lifting us out of poverty and offering the basics of life), the pursuit of wealth often makes us anxious, agitated, discontent, and lonely.

Perhaps this is why the bulk of Jesus' teachings on money are *warnings* about the danger of it, such as his cry in Luke 12v15:

> "Watch out! Be on your guard against all kinds of greed; life does not consist in an abundance of possessions."

In this session, we explore not just Jesus' warnings about wealth but also his invitation to a simpler life, marked by the biblical virtue of contentment. Again, we discover that Jesus' invitation to simplicity and generosity is an invitation to *joy*. Contentment itself is a way of being in which we are deeply happy with what we *have* and our life as it actually *is*, here and now.

We often believe the lie that we'll be happy when we "get"—a raise, a better job, a new home or car, etc.

The beautiful message of Jesus is that contentment cannot be bought, but it can be given.

Opening questions

01   What spontaneous act of generosity did you practice this week, and how did it go?

02   Were you able to feel the joy of God in your practice?

03   What challenges did you face emotionally, spiritually, or practically?

04   What new ideas about generosity have been growing in you this last week?

Teaching

Scripture

But godliness with contentment is great gain. For we brought nothing into the world, and we can take nothing out of it. But if we have food and clothing, we will be content with that. Those who want to get rich fall into temptation and a trap and into many foolish and harmful desires that plunge people into ruin and destruction. For the love of money is a root of all kinds of evil. Some people, eager for money, have wandered from the faith and pierced themselves with many griefs.

But you, man of God, flee from all this, and pursue righteousness, godliness, faith, love, endurance and gentleness. . . .

Command those who are rich in this present world not to be arrogant nor to put their hope in wealth, which is so uncertain, but to put their hope in God, who richly provides us with everything for our enjoyment. Command them to do good, to be rich in good deeds, and to be generous and willing to share. In this way they will lay up treasure for themselves as a firm foundation for the coming age, so that they may take hold of the life that is truly life.

—1 Timothy 6v6–11, 17–19

Session summary

- The majority of Jesus' teachings on money are warnings about the dangers of greed.

- Money is not neutral but powerful and difficult to steward well.

- The Practice of generosity is a two-sided coin where we determine both

  - what to give away.

  - how to live more simply.

- Contentment is a by-product of generosity.

- What we are searching for in money can be found only in God.

Teaching notes

As you watch Session 02 together, feel free to use this page to take notes.

Discussion questions

Now it's time for conversation about the teaching. Circle up in triads (groups of three). and discuss the following questions:

01 If you were to measure your level of contentment on a scale of 1 to 10—where 1 is feeling the anxiety of greed and a desire for more, and 10 is feeling non-anxious and satisfied with what you have—where would you plot yourself right now?

02 Where are you experiencing a lack of margin in your life? In your relationships, schedule, or finances?

03 What is one area in your life that you could possibly simplify (schedule, possessions, finances, etc.)?

04 Name some of the best things in your life right now. What are you most grateful for?

Practice notes

As you continue to watch Session 02 together, feel free to use this page to take notes.

Closing prayer

End your time together by praying this liturgy:

Giver of the present,
help us to be present too,
that in our joyful receiving
of the goodness we already have,
we may more richly welcome
the gift of our lives and your
unceasing presence amid them.

Practice

Our exercise for this week is based on Jesus' command: "Sell your possessions and give to the poor."* In context, he wasn't saying you need to sell everything. He was calling his followers to be the kinds of people who regularly simplify their lives, by selling their possessions and giving the money away to the poor.

Exercise: Identify something you own that you do not need. Give it away, or sell it and give the money to someone in need.

- **Identify an item to sell or give away.** You don't need to sell everything, just something. It could be an item you rarely use—that bike you never ride, the surfboard collecting dust, your aging record collection, etc. Or it could be an item you love and use regularly but feel the gentle pull of the Spirit to give away. This calls for prayerful discernment.

- **Give away the item or the money from its sale.** You can give to an organization like a local nonprofit or directly to someone who you know is in need. Don't make a big deal out of it. Just bless people as quietly as you can, without drawing attention to yourself or putting them in an awkward position. You may want to consider giving anonymously if you feel led to do so.

This exercise may be really hard and feel like peeling a layer off your heart, but on the other side is joy and freedom.

---

* Luke 12v33.

Reach Exercise: Simplify.

- **Pick a room, go through it thoughtfully and peacefully, and simplify it down to the essentials.** This could be your closet, bedroom, living room, kitchen, garage, etc.

- **As you quietly observe each item in the room, consider holding it up before God.**

- **Ask yourself questions:** *Do I really need this? Could I live without this? Would my life possibly be better without this unnecessary item?* Rather than asking ourselves how we can get more, we're pondering how we could live with less.

- **Make four piles for the unnecessary items:** (01) Throw away. (02) Recycle. (03) Sell. (04) Give away.

- **Give your extra stuff away.** You can give to the poor via The Salvation Army or a local donation drop, or give directly to someone you know.

- **Go sit in the decluttered room or area, and pay attention to how you feel.** Spend a few minutes in gratitude to God for the goodness of ordinary life.

To simplify your whole home and life is a long process that takes most people many weeks or months, but it can have a dramatic effect on your discipleship to Jesus, emotional well-being, and spiritual freedom. We've created a four-week guide to simplifying your life (available at practicingtheway.org), if you would like to pursue greater simplicity.

Additionally, you can listen to John Mark Comer's interviews with author, former pastor, and minimalist expert Joshua Becker:

- **Simplifying your wardrobe:**
  practicingthewayarchives.org/simplicity-practice/part-four
- **Simplifying your living room and bedrooms:**
  practicingthewayarchives.org/simplicity-practice/part-five
- **Simplifying your kitchen, bathrooms, and laundry:**
  practicingthewayarchives.org/simplicity-practice/part-five

You could also consider reading one of the following books:

- *Freedom of Simplicity* by Richard Foster

- *The More of Less* by Joshua Becker

- *Abundant Simplicity* by Jan Johnson

- *Essential* by the Minimalists

Go deeper

📖 Read

Giving Is the Good Life by Randy Alcorn
Chapters 05–08 (pages 61–110)

⑉ Listen

Rule of Life podcast on generosity
Episode 02

◎ Reflect

Before your next time together with the group for Session 03, take
10–15 minutes to journal your answers to the following three questions.

01 What aspect of simplifying did I find most difficult?

02 What emotions did I experience in simplifying and
giving away?

03 How do I sense the Spirit inviting me deeper into
simplicity going forward?

🗩 Discuss (Optional)

For those of you who would like to slow down and integrate this practice more deeply into your life, here is an optional group session you can do before you move on to Session 03 of this Practice.

Read this introduction

I can do all this through him who gives me strength.

—Philippians 4v13

Few verses in Scripture are more popular (and misunderstood) than these eleven words from Paul in his letter to the Philippian church. For Paul this was more than a motivational speech to roll up his sleeves and face life's circumstances; it was a statement about contentment in spite of them.

Many of us long to experience the content life, but it can feel elusive. We wait for a sense of contentment to trail behind the next thing: a raise, a promotion, keys to a home we can finally call ours. Yet contentment in Paul's experience was not derived from his circumstances but pronounced over them; it was not accumulated or purchased but discovered in Jesus and his Way.

In your time together today, we want you to give special attention to contentment, one of the more beautiful, counterintuitive by-products of a generous life in Christ.

Read this Scripture

I rejoiced greatly in the Lord that at last you renewed your concern for me. Indeed, you were concerned, but you had no opportunity to show it. I am not saying this because I am in need, for I have learned to be content whatever the circumstances. I know what it is to be in need, and I know what it is to have plenty. I have learned the secret of being content in any and every situation, whether well fed or hungry, whether living in plenty or in want. I can do all this through him who gives me strength.

Yet it was good of you to share in my troubles. Moreover, as you Philippians know, in the early days of your acquaintance with the gospel, when I set out from Macedonia, not one church shared with me in the matter of giving and receiving, except you only; for even when I was in Thessalonica, you sent me aid more than once when I was in need. Not that I desire your gifts; what I desire is that more be credited to your account. I have received full payment and have more than enough. I am amply supplied, now that I have received from Epaphroditus the gifts you sent. They are a fragrant offering, an acceptable sacrifice, pleasing to God. And my God will meet all your needs according to the riches of his glory in Christ Jesus.

To our God and Father be glory for ever and ever. Amen.

—Philippians 4v10–20

🗩 Discuss (Optional)

Discuss the text

01   Verse 13 is often misunderstood. How does your understanding of this verse change given the context of "content whatever the circumstances"?

02   What do you think is Paul's "secret" for a life of contentment?

03   Read Paul's overview of the persecution and trials he faced in 2 Corinthians 11v24–28. How does this impact your reading of the above passage, especially his contentment?

04   In the previous session, you provided a number on a scale of 1 to 10 to describe your level of contentment. If Paul's number is a 10, why do you think your numbers might be different or similar?

Discuss the Practice

01 Have you noticed any correlation in your own life between how much you own and how content you are? How does one impact the other?

02 In what ways do you notice the culture around you fostering discontentment in you?

03 Does it feel possible for you to have contentment regardless of your circumstances like Paul says? Why or why not?

04 In what ways, if any, did this week's exercise impact your view on material possessions and their role in your life?

All We Have Belongs to God

Overview

In the early pages of the Scriptures, a core claim is made about the universe, and alongside it we find a mandate for humanity. Simply put: Everything in the world belongs to God, and we are stewards of all he's put in it.

The Christian's identity as a steward underpins Jesus' invitation to the generous life. In God's world, we are not primarily savers or spenders, those who own or do not, but in a radical third take, we are caretakers— entrusted to do good with our resources, all of which belong to God. It is an entirely different lens through which to see the figures in our accounts and the possessions under our roofs.

While our previous session highlighted contentment in *what we already have*, this session invites us to ask the next natural question: *Now how will we use it?*

Opening questions

When instructed, pause the video for a few minutes to discuss in small groups:

01 What did your practice of generosity look like
this week?

02 What has it looked like to invite God into your
current framework of generosity? How has he led
you or invited you to be generous in a new way?

03 Where have you noticed the influence of greed in
your own life this week, and what might you need
to confess to God or others in light of that?

04 When it comes to simplicity and generosity, what
internal or external obstacles are you facing?

Teaching

Scripture

"Be dressed ready for service and keep your lamps burning, like servants waiting for their master to return from a wedding banquet, so that when he comes and knocks they can immediately open the door for him. It will be good for those servants whose master finds them watching when he comes. Truly I tell you, he will dress himself to serve, will have them recline at the table and will come and wait on them. It will be good for those servants whose master finds them ready, even if he comes in the middle of the night or toward daybreak. But understand this: If the owner of the house had known at what hour the thief was coming, he would not have let his house be broken into. You also must be ready, because the Son of Man will come at an hour when you do not expect him."

Peter asked, "Lord, are you telling this parable to us, or to everyone?"

The Lord answered, "Who then is the faithful and wise manager, whom the master puts in charge of his servants to give them their food allowance at the proper time? It will be good for that servant whom the master finds doing so when he returns. Truly I tell you, he will put him in charge of all his possessions. But suppose the servant says to himself, 'My master is taking a long time in coming,' and he then begins to beat the other servants, both men and women, and to eat and drink and get drunk. The master of that servant will come on a day when he does not expect him and at an hour he is not aware of. He will cut him to pieces and assign him a place with the unbelievers.

"The servant who knows the master's will and does not get ready or does not do what the master wants will be beaten with many blows. But the one who does not know and does things deserving punishment will be beaten with few blows. From everyone who has been given much, much will be demanded; and from the one who has been entrusted with much, much more will be asked."

—Luke 12v35–48

Session summary

- Scripture encourages us to see wealth through the lens of stewardship, not ownership.

- The three components of a biblical theology of stewardship are:

  - God owns it all.

  - We are entrusted by God with his resources to do good.

  - God blesses us to give more, not just to have more.

- We are invited to discern with the Spirit what stewardship looks like for each of us in our particular season and circumstance.

- A key practice to this end is learning to listen to God's voice about money and generosity.

Teaching notes

As you watch Session 03 together, feel free to use these pages to take notes.

Discussion questions

01 What emotions surface in you as you consider Jesus' parable of the faithful and wise manager? How does it encourage you, and how does it challenge you?

02 In your family of origin, what were the views and emotional dispositions toward money? In what ways have those shaped your relationship to money today?

03 Share about a time when you asked God about a financial decision in your life and listened for his direction.

04 How could the truth that everything belongs to God free you to live more generously?

Practice notes

As you continue to watch Session 03 together, feel free to use this page to take notes.

Closing prayer

End your time together by praying this liturgy:

Holy Spirit, help us to see
all we have as God's,
including our very selves,
that we may learn the power
and the joy of living like
we've nothing to lose,
yet everything to gain,
in you.

Practice

Exercise: Begin listening to God about money and generosity.

- Find a quiet, distraction-free place, and put away your phone and devices.

- Center yourself in God: Take a few deep, slow breaths, ground yourself in the moment, and become aware of God's presence all around you.

- Ask the Holy Spirit to come and guide your mind into his will for your finances and future.

- Then journal through the prompts on the next pages.

Imagine living a generous life

Take a moment to imagine living without financial anxiety or discontent. What would it feel like? What would you experience when opening your banking app? Or when an opportunity to meet a need came along?

Name the financial worries that stand between you and that peaceful place.

_____

_____

_____

_____

_____

Name any unsated desires that are driving you away from generosity (and are causing greed, discontent, etc.).

_____

_____

_____

_____

_____

Name whatever practical obstacles keep you from living a more generous life (debt, a car payment, unemployment, etc.).

_____

_____

_____

_____

_____

Identify the lies that keep you from living a generous life

What lies do I believe about God's ability or willingness to provide for my needs?

_____

_____

_____

_____

Where did each lie come from (a childhood experience, word from an authority figure, etc.)?

_____

_____

_____

_____

What is the truth? (Consider Philippians 4v19 or 2 Corinthians 9v11.)

_____

_____

_____

_____

How would my financial life change if I started living into the truth over the lie?

_____

_____

_____

_____

You may want to pause here and slowly read Psalm 23, replacing your name for every "I" and "me"—such as "The LORD is Sarah's shepherd. Sarah lacks nothing . . ." Read it prayerfully, and meditate on God as your shepherd and yourself being led and cared for perfectly.

Identify what you have to give

The first step toward generosity is not necessarily giving your money away. The first discipline is bringing order. If your finances are chaotic, you don't really know what you have (or don't have) to give.

Proverbs 27v23 says, "Be sure you know the condition of your flocks, give careful attention to your herds." In the ancient Near East, wealth was measured not in investments and brokerage accounts but in land and flocks and herds. Land was easy to measure. You knew what you had. But flocks and herds took a little more work. You had to walk out in the field, then count them and make sure they were healthy. So Proverbs invites us to pay attention: Know what you have. Don't obsess on it, and don't give yourself anxiety by watching every market fluctuation, but know what's going on.

Take a moment to list some of the financial and material possessions ("flocks and herds") God has gifted to you.

_____

_____

_____

_____

_____

_____

_____

_____

Note: We recommend you list both income (from your job or another source) and assets (such as a home or investments or possessions). We'd also recommend you calculate your "disposable income," whatever you have left after your basic expenses are covered.

Imagine a new future

Some things that God gives into our lives are for us. Some of us may accidentally dishonor God's generosity by not receiving the gifts he wants to give us. If a father gives a bike to his son for Christmas, he'd be a bit dismayed to see him pawning it, misusing it, or even giving it away.

The problem is that most of us just assume that whatever we have is for our consumption. The key question of formation regarding generosity that we must learn to ask is, "God, what's for me to enjoy? And what's for me to share?"

Jesus called the evil one a "thief," meaning he wants to steal God's gifts from us and others. "The thief comes only to steal and kill and destroy."*

What's the opposite of stealing? Giving. What's the opposite of killing? Living. And what's the opposite of destroying? Building.

Give, live, and build. These are three healthy outlets for our finances. Some of our finances are for us to give away; some are to live on and even to deeply enjoy our lives before God; and some are to build for the future God has put in our hearts and his callings on our lives.

Take a moment to think about your finances through this threefold rubric of give/live/build.

---

* John 10v10.

What do you give (to others, the church, the poor)?

What do you live on (shelter, food, healthcare, transportation, etc.)?

What do you build with (savings, investments, retirement, your business, debt reduction, etc.)?

_____ _____ _____

_____ _____ _____

_____ _____ _____

_____ _____ _____

_____ _____ _____

_____ _____ _____

_____ _____ _____

_____ _____ _____

_____ _____ _____

_____ _____ _____

_____ _____ _____

_____ _____ _____

_____ _____ _____

_____ _____ _____

Now, begin to listen to God

Take a few deep breaths, and invite the Holy Spirit to fill your mind and heart. Just quietly wait after each prompt for the Spirit to bring to your imagination any thoughts or feelings or desires he has for you.

God, is there anything about my current stewardship (giving, living, or building) that you want me to change?

Do you want me to give differently?

Do you want me to live differently?

Do you want me to build differently?

If you've genuinely asked the Spirit to speak over your life and you sense peace over the way things are, enjoy your life with joy and contentment. But if you sense the Spirit moving you to change your budget or to give in a new way, move quickly to obey, and watch what happens in your heart and life.

As we follow Jesus, "surely [his] goodness and love will follow [us]."*

---

* Psalm 23v6.

Reach Exercise: Enjoy something good in your life, and share it with another.

The goal for this Reach Exercise is to pair sacrificial giving with deep enjoyment and celebration of the gift of life. In one of the apostle Paul's hallmark passages on money and generosity, he both commands the rich "to be generous and willing to share" and reminds them (and us) that God "richly provides us with everything for our enjoyment."*

The responsibility of generosity is designed to function best when held in tandem with the discipline of celebration.

Here are a few ideas to spark your imagination:

- Take someone out to a nice dinner.

- Open that bottle of wine you've been saving and share it with a good friend.

- Watch a sunset with your family and give thanks for your life.

- Take a kid from your community who doesn't have a healthy family situation out for ice cream.

- Cook a really good dinner and savor it with your family or friends.

- Throw a party to celebrate a milestone in your life or someone in your community.

- Go take in an art museum or public park with someone you love, and pay close, unhurried attention to beauty and goodness.

---

* 1 Timothy 6v17–18.

Go deeper

📖 Read

Giving Is the Good Life by Randy Alcorn
Chapters 09–12 (pages 111–166)

ḩᶅᶅᶅ Listen

Rule of Life podcast on generosity
Episode 03

◎ Reflect

Before your next time together with the group for Session 04, take
10–15 minutes to journal your answers to the following three questions.

01 Where did I feel resistance?

02 Which emotions did I expect to experience? Which
ones surprised me?

03 In what ways did I encounter God in this exercise?

🗩 Discuss (Optional)

For those of you who would like to slow down and integrate this practice more deeply into your life, here is an optional group session you can do before you move on to Session 04 of this Practice.

Read this introduction

In our various Practices, we have shared at length about how spiritual disciplines are not religious mechanisms to twist God's favor toward us or behavioral checkboxes on a Christian scorecard. Much more profoundly, they are ways we open up our deepest selves to be transformed by the life and love of the Trinity. The disciplines can ultimately transform our lives because they are portals for the Spirit to transform our hearts.

In today's passage from Ecclesiastes, the author invites us to take an honest journey into the subterranean movements of our inner lives: moving the magnifying glass from our behaviors around wealth to our love of it. This is perhaps one of the most important reflections we can undertake in this Practice of generosity, for in the poignant words often attributed to the Italian saint St. Clare of Assisi, "we become what we love."

Read this Scripture

Whoever loves money never
has enough;
whoever loves wealth is never
satisfied with their income.
This too is meaningless.

As goods increase,
so do those who consume them.
And what benefit are they to
the owners
except to feast their eyes on them?

The sleep of a laborer is sweet,
whether they eat little or much,
but as for the rich, their abundance
permits them no sleep.

I have seen a grievous evil
under the sun:

wealth hoarded to the harm of
its owners,
or wealth lost through some
misfortune,
so that when they have children
there is nothing left for them
to inherit.
Everyone comes naked from their
mother's womb,
and as everyone comes, so
they depart.

They take nothing from their toil
that they can carry in their hands.

This too is a grievous evil:

As everyone comes, so they depart,
and what do they gain,
since they toil for the wind?
All their days they eat in darkness,
with great frustration, affliction
and anger.

This is what I have observed to be
good: that it is appropriate for a
person to eat, to drink and to find
satisfaction in their toilsome labor
under the sun during the few days of
life God has given them—for this is
their lot. Moreover, when God gives
someone wealth and possessions, and
the ability to enjoy them, to accept
their lot and be happy in their toil—
this is a gift of God. They seldom
reflect on the days of their life,
because God keeps them occupied
with gladness of heart.

—Ecclesiastes 5v10–20

🗩 Discuss (Optional)

Here is how Randy Alcorn summarizes the wisdom in verses 10–15:

- v10: The more you have, the more you want.

- v10: The more you have, the less you're satisfied.

- v11: The more you have, the more people (including the government) will come after it.

- v11: The more you have, the more you realize it does you no good.

- v12: The more you have, the more you have to worry about.

- v13: The more you have, the more you can hurt yourself by holding onto it.

- v14: The more you have, the more you have to lose.

- v15: The more you have, the more you'll leave behind.

Discuss the text

01   In what ways have you seen the love of money negatively impact our world?

02   Pay attention to what the author of Ecclesiastes considers "grievous evil." How does the evil identified there differ from what might be deemed evil by our surrounding culture?

03   The line between making more money and beginning to love it can be difficult to spot. How do you think people can discern and avoid that trap?

04   Reread Randy Alcorn's summary of Ecclesiastes 5v10–15 on page 80. Which summary line most stands out to you and why?

Discuss the Practice

01   Do you see generosity primarily through the lens of sacrifice or joy? Why do you think that is?

02   How was your experience beginning this week's Practice with listening prayer? What did you sense the Spirit leading you toward?

03   Did you experience hesitancy or excitement in inviting God to speak directly to your generosity? Why?

04   If you are willing, share with the group part or all of your response to question 03 of your Practice Reflection on page 76.

Be Generous to the Poor

Overview

One of the most distinct characteristics of the earliest Christians was their disproportionate concern for the poor. While this may be a more common value in our day, Jesus' teachings about the poor were revolutionary to ancient Roman ears in a world built on "takers" and "keepers." Jesus flipped the hero's story of that time on its head and raised the disenfranchised into the eyeline of society.

When hearts are generally inclined toward *more* and *mine*, radical generosity to the poor is Jesus' way of setting us free to join him in his upside-down Kingdom that belongs to "the poor in spirit"* and "the least of these."**

---

* Matthew 5v3.
** Matthew 25v40.

Opening questions

When instructed, pause the video for a few minutes to discuss in small groups:

01 How did the truth that everything belongs to God free you to live more generously this week?

02 Did you sense God saying anything to you this week about the way you steward your resources?

03 What is one way that you lived as a "caretaker" this week? What did that look like?

04 One year from now, what do you want your life to look like with regard to money, simplicity, and generosity?

Teaching

Scripture

Someone in the crowd said to him, "Teacher, tell my brother to divide the inheritance with me."

Jesus replied, "Man, who appointed me a judge or an arbiter between you?" Then he said to them, "Watch out! Be on your guard against all kinds of greed; life does not consist in an abundance of possessions."

And he told them this parable: "The ground of a certain rich man yielded an abundant harvest. He thought to himself, 'What shall I do? I have no place to store my crops.'

"Then he said, 'This is what I'll do. I will tear down my barns and build bigger ones, and there I will store my surplus grain. And I'll say to myself, "You have plenty of grain laid up for many years. Take life easy; eat, drink and be merry."'

"But God said to him, 'You fool! This very night your life will be demanded from you. Then who will get what you have prepared for yourself?'

"This is how it will be with whoever stores up things for themselves but is not rich toward God."

Then Jesus said to his disciples: "Therefore I tell you, do not worry about your life, what you will eat; or about your body, what you will wear. For life is more than food, and the body more than clothes. Consider the ravens: They do not sow or reap, they have no storeroom or barn; yet God feeds them. And how much more valuable you are than birds! Who of you by worrying can add a single hour to your life? Since you cannot do this very little thing, why do you worry about the rest?

"Consider how the wild flowers grow. They do not labor or spin. Yet I tell you, not even Solomon in all his splendor was dressed like one of these. If that is how God clothes the grass of the field, which is here today, and tomorrow is thrown into the fire, how much more will he clothe you—you of little faith! And do not set your heart on what you will eat or drink; do not worry about it. For the pagan world runs after all such things, and your Father knows that you need them. But seek his kingdom, and these things will be given to you as well.

"Do not be afraid, little flock, for your Father has been pleased to give you the kingdom. Sell your possessions and give to the poor. Provide purses for yourselves that will not wear out, a treasure in heaven that will never fail, where no thief comes near and no moth destroys. For where your treasure is, there your heart will be also."

—Luke 12v13–34

Session summary

- A defining characteristic of a disciple of Jesus is their generosity to the poor.

- The poor are "anyone who [has] need"* around you.

- A core practice of the earliest Christians was almsgiving: the giving of money, time, and relationship to the poor.

- Jesus' teachings and the early church's example invite us to ask:

  ○ Who do I know is in need?

  ○ What do I have to give?

---

* Acts 2v45.

Teaching notes

Discussion questions

01 In what ways are you inspired by stories of radical generosity? In what ways do they challenge you?

02 In your everyday life, how often do you find yourself proximate to those on the margins of our society? What has it looked like to share your resources with them?

03 Who in your life has access to the way you steward your finances? And do they have permission to speak into it honestly? If not, whom could you invite into this space?

04 As we finish this Practice, what invitations to generosity do you sense the Spirit extending?

Practice notes

As you continue to watch Session 04 together, feel free to use this page to take notes.

Closing prayer

End your time together by praying this liturgy:

You have said, Jesus,
that the kingdom of heaven
belongs to the poor;
help us to orient ourselves
toward them as you do,
that in our loving how you love,
we may know you all the more.

Practice

Exercise: Be generous to the poor.

Our exercise for this week is to share your resources with someone in need. **You can give to an organization doing good work serving the poor, either globally or locally.**

Or you can give to someone who you know is in need in your relational circle. This could be a member of your extended family, someone in your community or church, or just someone you know of in your circle of reach.

If you give directly to someone you know, you could buy them groceries, send cash to help pay bills, purchase an item they need, or drop off money or necessary items at their home anonymously.

If you don't know what to do, pray for God to illuminate an idea in your heart and direct your steps into what is pleasing to him.

Reach Exercise: Give not just your money but your time.

If you see a need, meet it yourself.

This could look like serving dinner at your local rescue mission, mowing an elderly neighbor's lawn, mentoring a kid in your local school, or sharing a meal with someone on the margins. There are a thousand ways to express the love of Jesus.

The goal is to blur the lines between giver and receiver, to become kin and family of God.

Ways to give globally or locally

Around the world

Here are two great organizations that serve the poor worldwide:

- **Compassion International**

  Through Compassion's signature Sponsor a Child program, gifts of around $50 per month connect children in the developing world to the church, education, nutrition, mentoring, and medical care.

- **Hope International**

  Hope International disburses small loans (microloans) to help marginalized people around the world. Through savings group communities, Hope shares biblical truth and practical wisdom. Recipients repay the funds 98 percent of the time, allowing gifts to flow to more and more people in need. Consider sending $25 per month, which would invest in the dreams of one micro-entrepreneur each month.

In your community

Many churches have ways to jump in and connect with those in your local community. If your church doesn't have that, here are two faithful organizations to check out that may be working in your region:

- **Citygate Network**

  Citygate is a network of rescue missions that point people toward Jesus. If you're in North America, see if there's a place for you to consider both giving financially and getting involved personally.

- **The Salvation Army**

  Operating in more than 130 countries through thousands of local offices, The Salvation Army meets the physical, emotional, and spiritual needs of people through social services, disaster relief, and more.

Go deeper

📖 Read

Giving Is the Good Life by Randy Alcorn
Chapters 13–18, conclusion (pages 167–261)

ᯮ Listen

Rule of Life podcast on generosity
Episode 04

◎ Reflect

Before your next time together with the group for the Bonus Session, take 10–15 minutes to journal your answers to the following three questions.

01 Where did I feel resistance or overwhelm?

02 What aspects of this exercise felt natural or unnatural to me?

03 What did I sense God doing in me as I gave?

🗩 Discuss (Optional)

For those of you who would like to slow down and integrate this practice more deeply into your life, here is an optional group session you can do before you move on to the Bonus Session of this Practice.

Read this introduction

Hope was once described by a pastor as "strength borrowed from tomorrow for today." As humans, we are hope generators, constantly trying to borrow strength and security from all sorts of sources to get through life—some reliable and some . . . not so much. In today's passage, Paul highlights one of the more tempting but unreliable sources of security: wealth. With a pastoral urgency, Paul lovingly commands Timothy and those under his care not to place their hope in riches and the life they bring, inviting us to ask this question: On what foundation are we building our sense of hope?

Read this Scripture

Command those who are rich in this present world not to be arrogant nor to put their hope in wealth, which is so uncertain, but to put their hope in God, who richly provides us with everything for our enjoyment. Command them to do good, to be rich in good deeds, and to be generous and willing to share. In this way they will lay up treasure for themselves as a firm foundation for the coming age, so that they may take hold of the life that is truly life.

—1 Timothy 6v17–19

Discuss the text

01 Paul offers seven commands in this short teaching to the rich. See if you can name them.

02 In light of global inequality, who are the "rich" in our world? If this passage is for us, not "someone else," which of the seven commands you listed feels most personally convicting?

03 What might the world look like if people believed they could "lay up treasure for themselves" eternally? How would it be different than it is now?

04 What are the signs that someone has "put their hope in wealth"?

Discuss the Practice

01 How has this Practice revealed the ways you have put your "hope in wealth"?

02 Are you coming to believe the generous life is "truly life" as Paul says? Why or why not?

03 Paul adds another dimension to generosity here: "to be rich in good deeds." In what particular ways can you be generous beyond the giving of your money in this season of your life?

04 What patterns or themes have you noticed emerge as you live into more generosity?

Best Practices for Generosity

Overview

As we come to the end of our Generosity Practice, it is clear that a generous life will not be stumbled upon but must be strategized for; our world of advertisements and algorithms, and our hearts prone to greed and fear, create too strong an undertow.

What is most needed at this point is a plan: a way to thoughtfully integrate Jesus' teachings on this Practice into the rhythm of our lives.

In this session, we set out to answer a few practical questions you might still have and to invite you to consider some best practices for building an architecture that can house a life of generosity.

Teaching

Scripture

Do not wear yourself out to get rich;
   do not trust your own cleverness.
Cast but a glance at riches, and they are gone,
   for they will surely sprout wings
   and fly off to the sky like an eagle.

—Proverbs 23v4–5

Session summary

- If riches are sure to "sprout wings and fly off," a generous life will require a plan.

- Start being generous now, even if you start small.

- You can begin by giving toward these things:

  - The poor

  - The church

  - The advancing of the gospel

- While generosity will look different depending on class and culture, there are five best practices to live into Jesus' vision of the generous life:

  - Firstfruits

  - A generosity fund

  - Tithing

  - A graduated tithe

  - Radical class distinction

- Combat our cultural "money taboo" by engaging in communal conversations and practices of generosity.

IN COMMUNITY

Teaching notes

As you watch the Bonus Session together, feel free to use these pages to take notes.

Discussion questions

01 What has God done in your heart through
this Practice?

02 What have you changed in your life as a result of
learning about generosity?

03 What challenges continue to surface in your heart
when it comes to money and generosity?

04 Are there any next steps you sense God may
be leading you to take in regard to money and
generosity?

Practice notes

As you continue to watch the Bonus Session together, feel free to use this page to take notes.

Closing prayer

End your time together by praying this liturgy:

Where our hearts have shrunk,
and our giving with them,
Holy Spirit, come.
Silence

To the fears that restrain us
and our anxiety for material things,
Holy Spirit, come.
Silence

To our other-blindness
and the busyness that causes it,
Holy Spirit, come.
Silence

That we may overflow
in abundant generosity,
Holy Spirit, come.
Silence

That our giving may transform the
world,
the poor, the church, and us,
Holy Spirit, come.
Silence

That we may know you greatly
through the expansion of our offering,
Holy Spirit, come.
Silence

Father, you're the embodiment of
"giving is better than receiving,"
and we want to be like you.
We praise and love you,
honor and desire you,
with all our beings,
now and forever,
amen.

Practice

Exercise: Make a plan for regular giving.

If you want this Practice to be the springboard to becoming a generous person, then you will need more than good intentions; you will need a plan.

Here's a short exercise designed to help you prayerfully make a plan for generosity coming out of this Practice:

- Find a quiet, distraction-free place, and put away your phone and devices.
- Center yourself in God: Take a few deep, slow breaths, ground yourself in the moment, and become aware of God's presence all around you.
- Ask the Holy Spirit to come and guide your mind into his will for your finances and future.
- Then journal through the prompts on the following pages.

What steps do you need to take or obstacles do you need to overcome to begin practicing generosity (e.g., secure employment, make a budget, get out of debt, pay down credit cards, sell your car and buy a cheaper model in cash, talk with a therapist about your financial fears, etc.)?

_____

_____

_____

_____

The three primary objects of generosity in the New Testament writings are the church, the gospel, and the poor.
How do you feel led to give to your local church?

_____

_____

_____

_____

How do you feel led to give to advance the gospel of the kingdom of God?

_____

_____

_____

_____

What steps do you need to take to begin giving (e.g., set up automatic donations monthly, change your budget, research nonprofits, etc.)?

_____

_____

_____

_____

Of the five best practices named in this session, which one(s) do you feel your heart drawn to? (Circle all that apply.)

Firstfruits   A generosity fund   Tithing   A graduated tithe   Radical class distinction

How do you want to adopt this practice (e.g., set aside $50 a month for a generosity fund, begin tithing, stop eating out for lunch, etc.)?

Many followers of Jesus reach a point in their lives where they each set a "lifestyle cap," a standard of living they do not go above. This enables them to give the extra away to what the Spirit is stirring in their heart. Randy Alcorn says God blesses us "not to raise [our] standard of living but to raise [our] standard of giving."* If your basic needs are met, do you want to set a "cap" on your lifestyle? If so, what do you feel is a joyful, peaceful, and appropriate way of life for you and your family in this season?

Are there any other ideas or invitations you sense the Spirit bringing to your mind and heart as you process?

* Randy Alcorn, The Treasure Principle: Unlocking the Secret of Joyful Giving (New York: Multnomah, 2001), 77.

Reach Exercise: Do this in community.

- Do this session's exercise on your own, then share it with a trusted friend, mentor, or a few members of your community.
- Share your budget with them as well as your giving plan.
- Let them look it over and speak into your life.
- If they offer, do the same for them.
- Be encouraging and gentle with each other. This is a huge step for most people. Avoid judgment, rigid thinking, comparison, or envy. Do everything in love.

This will feel scary at first! And you should do it only with someone you really trust. But this is a powerful act of defiance against the god of mammon and a key step toward greater freedom and joy.

PART 03

Continue the Journey

Recommended Reading

Growing in generosity is a lifelong journey for most of us. We stay on the path; we need to keep our mind set on the beauty and possibility of becoming a generous disciple of Jesus. Here are some of our favorite books on generosity, for those of you who desire to learn more.

The Grace of Giving by John Stott

The Treasure Principle by Randy Alcorn

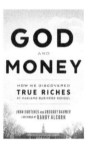

God and Money by Gregory Baumer and John Cortines

Joy Giving by Cameron Doolittle

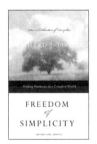

Freedom of Simplicity by Richard Foster

Abundant Simplicity by Jan Johnson

The More of Less by Joshua Becker

The Practices

Information alone isn't enough to produce transformation.

By adopting not just the teaching but the practices from Jesus' own life, we open up our entire beings to God and allow him to transform us into people of love.

Our nine core Practices work together to form a Rule of Life for the modern era.

Sabbath	Prayer	Fasting
Solitude	Generosity	Scripture
Community	Service	Witness

WHAT'S INCLUDED FOR EACH PRACTICE

Four Sessions
Each session includes teaching, guided discussion, and weekly exercises to integrate the Practices into daily life.

Companion Guide
A detailed guide provides question prompts, session-by-session exercises, and space to write and reflect.

Recommended Resources
Additional recommended readings and podcasts offer a way to get the most out of the Practices.

The Practicing the Way Course

An eight-session primer on spiritual formation

Two thousand years ago, Jesus said to his disciples, "Follow me." But what does it mean for us to follow Jesus today?

The Practicing the Way Course is an on-ramp to spiritual formation, exploring what it means to follow Jesus and laying the foundation for a life of apprenticeship to him.

WHAT'S INCLUDED

Eight Sessions

John Mark and other voices teaching on apprenticing under Jesus, spiritual formation, healing from sin, meeting God in pain, crafting a Rule of Life, living in community, and more

Exercises

Weekly practices and exercises to help integrate what you've learned into your everyday life

Guided Conversation

Prompts to reflect on your experience and process honestly in community

Companion Guide

A detailed workbook with exercises, space to write and reflect, and suggestions for supplemental resources

The Circle

Practicing the Way is a nonprofit that develops spiritual formation resources for churches and small groups learning how to become apprentices in the Way of Jesus.

We believe one of the greatest needs of our time is for people to discover how to become lifelong disciples of Jesus. To that end, we help people learn how to be with Jesus, become like him, and do as he did, through the practices and rhythms he and his earliest followers lived by.

All of our downloadable ministry resources are available at no cost, thanks to the generosity of The Circle and other givers from around the world who partner with us to see formation integrated into the church at large.

To learn more or join us, visit practicingtheway.org/give.

APPENDIX

For Facilitators

Before you begin, there are three easy things you need to do (this should take only 10–15 minutes).

01   Go to practicingtheway.org, log in, create a group, and send a digital invitation to your community.

02   Encourage your group to bring their Companion Guides to each session, as they contain the discussion questions and space to take notes.

- You can purchase a print or ebook version from your preferred book retailer or find a free digital PDF version at practicingtheway.org. We recommend the print version so you can stay away from your devices during the Practices, as well as take notes during each session. But we realize that digital works better for some.
- Note: You can order the Guides ahead of time and have them waiting when people arrive for Session 01 (see the final page of this book for bulk ordering information), or encourage people to order or download their own and bring them to your gatherings.

03   Send a message to your group encouraging everyone to take the Spiritual Health Reflection before your first gathering: practicingtheway.org/reflection.

For more resources for facilitating the Generosity Practice, we offer training videos at practicingtheway.org.

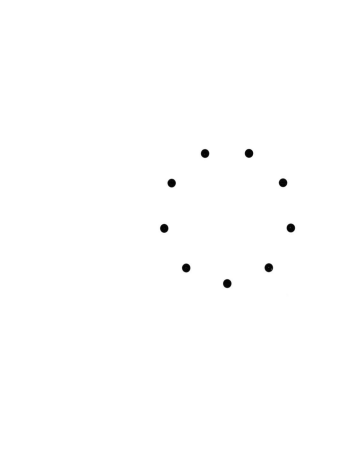

To inquire about ordering this Companion Guide in
bulk quantities for your church, small group, or staff,
contact churches@penguinrandomhouse.com.